Jane Austen
A Celebration

Also from Carcanet

Collected Poems and verse of the Austen family
edited by David Selwyn

Jane Austen
A Celebration

❧

Edited by Maggie Lane and David Selwyn

with a Foreword by
HRH The Prince of Wales

For Edward

from

David .

Worcester College,
30th May 2001 .

Fyfield Books

in association with the Jane Austen Society
and Chawton House Library

First published in Great Britain in 2000 by
Carcanet Press Limited
4th Floor, Conavon Court
12–16 Blackfriars Street
Manchester M3 5BQ

A CIP catalogue record for this book
is available from the British Library.
ISBN 1 85754 457 9

The Jane Austen Society acknowledges the support of the
Hampshire County Council in the publication of this book.

Supported by
Hampshire
County
Council

Set in 11pt Monotype Bell by XL Publishing Services, Tiverton
Printed and bound in England by SRP Ltd, Exeter

Contents

❦

In surveying the achievements of mankind over the last two thousand years, I believe that one of the most valuable contributions which Britain has made to the world is through our rich and varied literature. In drama - and not just Shakespeare - in poetry and in the novel, our great writers have explored all kinds of experience in language of extraordinary subtlety and beauty. They have thereby enriched immeasurably the lives of us all.

The novels of Jane Austen stand at the very peak of our literary heritage. Through the delightful comedy of their incomparable characters, the wit and elegance with which they are written and, above all, the profound understanding that they reveal of both the human heart and the human mind, they speak with freshness and wisdom to each new generation of readers.

I am delighted to lend my support to this volume commemorating the writings of Jane Austen. Her ability to continue to give pleasure to countless numbers of her readers could not be a better cause for celebration!

Jane lies in Winchester – blessed be her shade!
Praise the Lord for making her, and her for all she made!
And while the stones of Winchester, or Milsom Street,
remain,
Glory, love, and honour unto England's Jane!

RUDYARD KIPLING

Introduction

❦

The year 2000 seems a good time – though perhaps no better than any other – to celebrate Jane Austen. As we enter the third millennium, no figure in English Literature, with the exception of Shakespeare, stands higher in critical esteem or public affection. Her six major novels are studied and read the world over and through adaptations in film and television reach ever wider audiences. Her letters are relished both for their liveliness and wit and for the picture they give of the author and her times. Biographies proliferate. Societies in her honour flourish in Britain and abroad. She is discussed in conferences and dayschools; devotees track her down in Hampshire, Kent and Bath; she is 'merchandised' on teeshirts, mugs, pencils, keyrings, and notepads (the latter invariably called a 'little bit of ivory'); and her image, in her sister Cassandra's rather amateurish portrait, is more immediately recognisable than that of any other writer except, again, Shakespeare. She has become, in effect, a figure that inhabits our consciousness quite separately from her works, an embodiment of Regency manners very different from the subversive commentator on a money-dominated society portrayed by some fashionable academics. As a result of the extraordinary amount of attention that has been paid to her in this century by critics on the one hand and popularisers on the other, she is now both an object of intense critical scrutiny and a part of the heritage industry.

The affectionately regarded figure who transcends both her period and her writing may perhaps be said to date from

1924, when Kipling published his story 'The Janeites', in which there is a secret society dedicated to her, with the password *'Tilniz an' trap-doors'*. 'Jane?' says brother Humberstall, Freemason and hairdresser, formerly of the Royal Garrison Artillery. 'Why, she was a little old maid 'oo'd written 'alf a dozen books about a hundred years ago. 'Twasn't as if there was anythin' *to* 'em, either. *I* know. I had to read 'em.' Humberstall had been introduced to the Society of the Janeites during the war, and he recalls chalking up names of her characters on three of the guns: 'The Reverend Collins', 'General Tilney' and 'The Lady Catherine De Bugg'. 'Well,' he says, 'it's a very select Society, an' you've got to be a Janeite in your 'eart, or you won't have any success… I read all her six books now for pleasure 'tween times in the shop; an' it brings it all back – down to the smell of the glue-paint on the screens. You take it from me, Brethren, there's no one to touch Jane when you're in a tight place. Gawd bless 'er, whoever she was.' There must be many people who would endorse Humberstall's opinion, and some of them are to be found in this volume.

The aim of *Jane Austen: A Celebration* is to offer a view of what Jane Austen means to people who have distinguished themselves in various walks of life. Some of the comments are taken from published writings, others came in response to an invitation to contribute to the book and have been written specially for it. Academic literary criticism has for the most part been avoided, since it is readily and copiously available elsewhere. Instead it is the personal response that we have sought – the instinctive judgement or the telling anecdote which conveys the particular significance that Jane Austen has for the writer. In this way we hope to reflect not only the great diversity of people's views about her, but also what such views reveal about themselves, since, as the critic Lionel Trilling once observed, the responses to Jane Austen's work are nearly as interesting and important as the work itself; in trying to decide for or against her, he said, the reader is required to make 'no mere literary judgment but a decision about his own character and personality, and about his relation to society and all of life'. We hope, therefore, that additional enjoyment will be found in this book for what it reveals about the personalities and tastes of the contributors.

In soliciting comments and choosing quotations, it was decided to restrict sources to this century and this country. There is, of course, much affection and esteem for Jane Austen abroad, but a line had to be drawn somewhere, and it seemed reasonable to set out to see how she is regarded by her own countrymen today. As it turned out, even within these limitations, a surprisingly wide variety of people have had something of interest to say about her, whether specifically, or in other contexts, in essays, letters or diaries. Consequently, however different the writers themselves may be from one another, in making a response to Jane Austen they can be seen to have had something in common. Thus it was not only high political office that Harold Macmillan, reading *Pride and Prejudice* while he waited to see if he was to become Prime Minister, shared with Sir Winston Churchill, who had found solace in the same book when suffering from pneumonia during the height of the war. Similarly, D.H. Lawrence and Philip Larkin both invoked Jane Austen in a negative way to encourage aspiring novelists (Larkin claimed that he would rather read a new Barbara Pym than a new Jane Austen, but he *was* writing to Miss Pym at the time).

The alphabetical ordering of the passages, which seemed the most natural way of organising the book, created some interesting juxtapositions and contradictions. For example, Arnold Bennett's incautious assertion that Jane Austen did not know enough of the world to be a great novelist is followed a couple of pages later by Elizabeth Bowen's tart observation that it is only the very stupid who believe that life 'with the lid off' is more interesting than life with the lid on, and a little later still by Lord David Cecil's comment that her comprehensive and searching view of human nature 'invests her achievement with a universal character'. Bennett's view is very much a minority one, especially in more recent years (though the Lyttleton–Hart-Davis correspondence contained some amusingly unfashionable abuse); on the other hand, his objections to the 'Janeites' are echoed elsewhere – for example by William Plomer, who refers to their 'smirking and making masonic grimaces at one another'.

Another kind of contrast results from the fact that no attempt has been made to impose a uniform number of words on the contributors. Some have been brief and pithy (Sebastian Coe, Ranulph Fiennes, Margaret Forster); others – particularly those such as Joan Austen-Leigh and Tom Carpenter who have a personal connection with Jane Austen – have been more expansive. It is hoped that the varying lengths of the passages will add to the attractions of the book, and make it easier to dip into. Similarly, there is no house style: contributions have been printed in the form in which they were received, with explanatory foot-notes added where they are helpful. Sources of extracts are given on the page, with date of publication (though that may not necessarily be the same as the date of writing); further details will be found in the 'Acknowledgements'. If no source is supplied, the passage was written specially for the book.

One last point is worth making. The nomenclature of women writers has traditionally been problematical. None of Jane Austen's novels was published under her name during her lifetime: *Sense and Sensibility* had 'By a Lady' on the title page and subsequent books were described as being 'By the Author of ...' It is interesting to see the ways in which she has been referred to in the course of this century. To the Janeites, she was of course simply 'Jane', a form she herself never used, even when writing to her beloved sister. More formally, to E.M. Forster she was 'Miss Austen', rather as if he were expecting to receive her for tea in his rooms at King's College, Cambridge. The accepted way of referring to her, as it is to women novelists generally, is to use both names rather more frequently than would be the case with a man; this, however, has found less favour in recent years, when the somewhat curt-sounding 'Austen' has been employed, particularly in academic criticism. One of the contributors here even calls her 'Ms Austen' – a title which, in its deliberate blurring of marital distinctions, would surely have caused her considerable amusement. In whatever way she is thought of, we hope that this book will give pleasure, and that it will send the reader back to favourite passages in the novels – which is, after all, the very best way of celebrating Jane Austen.

MAGGIE LANE, DAVID SELWYN

Kingsley Amis
novelist

❦

It must be said at once that [*Mansfield Park*] succeeds brilliantly whenever it aims to hold up viciousness of character as vicious. Mrs Norris is very fully visualised in domestic and social terms, but these are the lineaments of a moral repulsiveness, and it is a superb if unintentional stroke of moral irony whereby she alone shows charity towards the disgraced and excommunicated Maria. Sir Thomas, again, represents an essay, carried out with scrupulous justice, in the case of the humane and high-principled man whose defects of egoism and a kind of laziness (to be seen running riot in the character of the wife) betray him into inhumanity and are shown as instrumental in the disasters visited upon his daughters. More important still, the unworthiness of Henry and Mary Crawford is allowed to emerge with an effect of inevitability that is only heightened by the author's freedom, almost audacity, in stressing their sprightliness and even their considerable share of right feeling. This is an achievement which changes in ethical outlook have left undimmed and which testifies to a unique and enviable moral poise.

All these, however, are relative triumphs. The characters mentioned, especially the Crawfords, exist less in their own right than in order to show up by contrast the central pair, not only in the status of persons but as embodiments of rival ideologies and ways of life. In both capacities the hero and heroine are deficient. The fact that as social beings they are inferior to the Crawfords, that Henry and Mary

1

are good fun and the other two aren't, is a very large part of the author's theme and is perfectly acceptable, even though this particular disparity sometimes goes too far for comfort and further, one cannot help feeling, than can have been intended: to invite Mr and Mrs Edmund Bertram round for the evening would not be lightly undertaken. More basically than this, Edmund and Fanny are both morally detestable and the endorsement of their feelings and behaviour by the author – an endorsement only withdrawn on certain easily recognisable occasions – makes *Mansfield Park* an immoral book.

'What Became of Jane Austen?', *Spectator*, 4 October 1957

W.H. Auden
poet

❧

She was not an unshockable blue-stocking;
    If shades remain the characters they were,
No doubt she still considers you as shocking.
    But tell Jane Austen, that is, if you dare,
    How much her novels are beloved down here.
She wrote them for posterity, she said;
'Twas rash, but by posterity she's read.

You could not shock her more than she shocks me;
    Beside her Joyce seems innocent as grass.
It makes me most uncomfortable to see
    An English spinster of the middle class
    Describe the amorous effects of 'brass',
Reveal so frankly and with such sobriety
The economic basis of society.

Letter to Lord Byron, 1937

3

Joan Austen-Leigh

descendant of Jane Austen's eldest brother and
founder of the Jane Austen Society of North America

❦

When I was a child, my father Lionel Austen-Leigh
explained to me that when *he* was a child his father, the Rev.
Arthur Austen-Leigh – vicar of Wargrave, fourth of the
eight sons of James Edward Austen-Leigh – brought him
up to believe that because Jane Austen was his ancestor, he
was, so to speak, not like other, ordinary mortals. A Very
Bad Thing, declared my father, shaking his head.

Curious. Because I was brought up exactly the same way.

For many years, however this sense of being anointed,
as it were, availed me nothing. I was born and still live in
a small city on the west coast of Canada. In vain did I put
up my hand in class, as I distinctly remember doing, to
announce with pride, 'Jane Austen is my great great great
aunt'. Like Emma, I was silenced. In the 1920s and 1930s
Jane Austen was quite unknown among my schoolfellows.
No doubt my parents' friends – all British – had read Jane
Austen. But in those days children did not eat with their
parents. At least my sister and I didn't. It was not infre-
quently drawn to our attention that we were both supposed
to be boys.

At sixteen I was dispatched to England to live with my
father's sisters, Honor and Lois Austen-Leigh. There, I was
deemed sufficiently civilised to dine with the adults. In my
aunts' house, originally named 'Sanditon', the honoured
name of Jane Austen was often invoked. Reference was also
made to great aunt Mary Austen-Leigh whom Honor and

4

Lois had known well, visiting at her home, Hartfield, Roehampton, where she lived with her brother William and where Jane Austen was the centre of their lives. Mary wrote *Personal Aspects of Jane Austen*, and William, with his nephew, R.A. Austen-Leigh, produced the first definitive biography, *Life and Letters of Jane Austen.*

My aunts used to talk of Jane Austen's characters, not at all in an academic way, but simply as living people one knew as friends. One question which exercised my aunt Honor most grievously: would Mr Woodhouse have allowed Mr Knightley and Emma to open the windows of their bedroom at night?

At my aunts' house, daily life was filled with Jane Austen. To them, a thank-you letter was always a collins, and in the drawing-room, on the grand piano, reposed Jane's very own writing-box[1] for any visitor to touch and see. Paradoxically, it was treated both as a sacred relic as well as an ordinary household object which had as much right to be there as the silver candlesticks on the dining-room table adorned with the crest of the Leigh Perrots. Little did I think, at the time, that these objects would one day descend to me. My aunt Lois published detective novels and my aunt Honor played the viola well enough to take part in string quartets with professional musicians who came to tea. One of their friends was Sir Frank McKinnon, a retired judge, author of *Grand Larceny*, the trial of Jane Leigh Perrot, which he dedicated to my aunts.

From these cultured and cultivated surroundings, upon the advent of Munich, I was summarily ejected and shipped back to Canada. At nineteen, I married, moved to a small logging village and spent the next twenty-five years raising four children and working in my husband's business. Jane Austen? Forget it!

1. Now presented by Joan Austen-Leigh and her daughters to the British Library.

I continued to read her books, however, and from time to time we travelled to England to attend meetings in the tent of the Jane Austen Society. That was in the days of Sir Hugh Smiley, Lord David Cecil and Chawton Cottage.

Then, in 1975, the bicentenary of Jane Austen's birth occurred, and my life was forever changed.

At a costume ball held at Oakley Hall, where Jane Austen had once visited Mrs Bramston and eaten 'sandwiches all over mustard', I met J. David (Jack) Grey from New York City. He was the first person I had ever encountered in my entire life – and I was at that time fifty-five years old – who knew as much, or more, than I did about Jane Austen and who loved and venerated her as I did.

It is hard to believe in these days when movie and television adaptations abound and Jane even has her own web site, that twenty-five years ago she was so very little known to the general public. Jack Grey and I were ecstatic to discover, each in the other, a fellow addict. It was my husband Denis Mason Hurley who suggested – no, badgered – Jack and me to found our own society on our side of the Atlantic. At first we balked, asserting that neither of us cared for groups or joining things. Four years later, in 1979, together with Henry Burke, we founded the Jane Austen Society of North America (JASNA). The first meeting took place in New York City at the Gramercy Park Hotel. Three hundred and fifty members had already joined. Twenty years on, there are 3,500.

Now, at last, my relationship to my aunt Jane Austen had tangible meaning. Since that memorable day she has become the central focus of my life. JASNA has brought me and many others unimagined pleasure and stimulating, far-flung friendships.

In my observation, Jane Austen, is a connector, a catalyst, joining like-minded people. You meet. You're drawn together. In due course you probably find that you also

6

both like Virginia Woolf, Evelyn Waugh and E.F. Benson. From an initially Austen-inspired friendship a whole range of subjects and interests develop.

Of course I am very proud of belonging to Jane. And – dare I admit it? thinking of my father – there's a faint feeling of smugness, of superiority, even, at having – as a Los Angeles acquaintance once put it – JA's DNA running through one's veins.

I have remarked that my sister and I were both expected to be boys. Since we were not, we are , alas, the last of the Austen-Leighs. (Of what use is it to have eight sons, if, in two generations, the name dies out?) Were we living in the nineteenth century my descendants would have changed their names. Almost none of the Chutes of the Vyne were born with the name. The rule was simple. You inherited the Vyne. You became a Chute – often collaterally, some-times by marriage, and sometimes through the female line. This information is not entirely irrelevant. Mrs Chute's niece, Emma Smith, became the wife of James Edward Austen-Leigh.

My daughters have not had the advantage of being born Austen-Leighs. Nevertheless, they feel 'very properly' towards their ancestor. One says she likes 'the fact that my family's roots can be traced back for so many generations…'. Another speaks of 'enjoying a sip of the soup from a spoon Jane may have used …'. A third remarks, 'When my son writes well I can't help but think it's Jane's genes percolating down …'.

A grandson, aged fifteen, declares, 'It's kind of neat.'

My own inner feeling is that wars, earthquakes, torna-does and disasters may overtake the world, but one fixed point remains – a light that never goes out, a centre that always holds – to be invoked in happiness or in sorrow: Jane Austen.

John Bayley
Professor of English Literature

🍂

To a book lover there is something slightly disquieting today about the way in which television has ingested not only the literary classics, from Jane Austen to *The Last of the Mohicans*, but the whole spectrum of reading matter. Not so much for its own immediate purposes as spectacle, but by a sort of divine right as top artistic medium, exercising an ultimate control over the circulation and popularity of the bookish world. Sales of Jane Austen notoriously shot up after the televising of *Pride and Prejudice* and *Persuasion*; and many readers have found – I experienced it myself – that their own private sense of the image and tone of these books had been affected, though we may hope not irreparably, by a purely visual imprint now imposed on the reading surface of the mind. Jane Austen's words and sentences, creating Elizabeth and Mr Darcy and the others, had been overprinted by their screen images, losing all their verbal subtlety in the process.

'Other Worlds to Inhabit' in *A Passion for Books*, 1999

Quentin Bell

artist and writer

❦

Was it on the same weekend that I argued with Bunny [David Garnett] about Jane Austen? Bunny had great admiration for the novels, but he had strong reservations on the subject of *Emma*. Emma he maintained was a very unpleasant character, a desperate snob, callous, conceited and vain. There was nothing to be said for her. I replied that although she had her faults she did suffer from an unbearably silly father and that she bore his silliness with exemplary patience.

For a moment Bunny was at a loss, but he was not a man who could easily be put down, and he responded, almost seriously: 'Well, we've only got Jane Austen's word for it'. Which is, I suppose the highest praise that one can give a novelist.

Elders and Betters, 1995

9

Alan Bennett
playwright

❧

Fans are a feature of a certain kind of book. It's often a children's book – *Winnie the Pooh*, *Alice* and *The Hobbit* are examples – or it is a grown-up children's book such as those of Wodehouse, E.F. Benson and Conan Doyle. But Jane Austen and Anthony Trollope are nothing if not adult and they have fans too – so children are not the essence of it.

What is common to all these authors, though, is the capacity to create self-contained worlds; their books constitute systems of literary self-sufficiency in ways that other novels, often more profound, do not. It is a kind of cosiness.

The Preface to *The Wind in the Willows* in *Writing Home*, 1994

Arnold Bennett
novelist

❦

Jane Austen? I feel that I am approaching dangerous ground. The reputation of Jane Austen is surrounded by cohorts and defenders who are ready to do murder for their sacred cause. They are nearly all fanatics. They will not listen. If anybody 'went for' Jane, anything might happen to him. He would assuredly be called on to resign from his clubs. I would sooner perjure myself. On the other hand I do not want to 'go for' Jane. I like Jane. I have read several Janes more than once. And in the reading of Jane's novels there happens to be that which can only happen in the work of a considerable author. I mean that first you prefer one novel, then you prefer another novel, and so on. Time was when I convinced myself that *Persuasion* was her masterpiece, with *Emma* a good second. Now I am inclined to join the populace and put *Pride and Prejudice* in the front, with *Mansfield Park* a good second.

But listening to the more passionate Janites (and among them are some truly redoubtable persons) one receives the impression that in their view Jane and Shakespeare are the only two English authors who rightly count, and that Shakespeare is joined with her chiefly as a concession to the opinion of centuries. I do not subscribe to this heated notion. I do not even agree that Jane was a great novelist. She was a great little novelist. She is marvellous, intoxicating: she has unique wit, vast quantities of common sense, a most agreeable sense of proportion, much narrative skill. And she is always readable.

11

But her world is a tiny world, and even of that tiny world she ignores, consciously or unconsciously, the fundamental factors. She did not know enough of the world to be a great novelist. She had not the ambition to be a great novelist. She knew her place; her present 'fans' do not know her place, and their antics would without doubt have excited Jane's lethal irony. I should say that either Emily or Charlotte Brontë was a bigger novelist than Jane.

'Books and Persons', *Evening Standard*, 21 July 1927

Mr Walpole misspells the glorious name of Jane Austen's 'Elizabeth Bennett'. A man capable of this appalling deed would be capable of assassinating his grandmother.

Ibid., 17 May 1928

Rachel Billington
novelist

❦

I first read Jane Austen when I was thirteen and I thought she was a romantic novelist. By turns I fell in love with Darcy, Captain Wentworth and Mr Knightley – although at nearly forty he was a little old for my tastes. In my twenties I changed tack and read Austen as a comic novelist, all wit and no heart. In my thirties I turned against her, citing her obsession with money and her snobbery.

Fortunately, when I was approached to write a sequel to *Emma*[1] I had combined all these reactions. She wrote about love, I had decided, not excluding sexual love, and about money and the makings of society – which made her perfectly in tune with our modern preoccupations. It was no surprise to me when she topped the ratings round the world. Film producers and television moguls had merely recognised an obvious winner.

Nor did I disapprove of the idea that a reader or viewer, hooked on the wonderful cast of characters, should be presented with an extension to their lives written by another pen. There are no rules in the making of art – artists as distant from each other as Shakespeare and Benjamin Britten pick up other people's characters and make them their own.

However many millions of people round the world read, watch or listen to Jane Austen, it is the love story that will hold and attract the majority. Each of her novels is cast

1. *Perfect Happiness*, 1998

round the progression of a young woman's search for love and happiness in marriage.

Jane Austen never made a married couple her central characters, unlike, for example, George Eliot. I was presented with a strange contradiction: an author who made marriage a happy ending but who describes the institution, once underway, with a very sceptical eye. This seems good reason why Jane Austen might be so popular an author at the moment, combining just what our age seems to want: a strong romantic sensibility with a deeply cynical sense of realism.

If there is one aspect of Jane Austen's genius that overwhelms all others it is her invention of characters. They have a living, breathing roundness to them which makes them, even when nearest to caricature such as Lady Catherine de Bourgh or Miss Bates, utterly convincing. It is this gift, in particular, which makes the translation to screen so successful. I had always admired the depiction of the slightly (or more than slightly) caddish figures of the Wickhams, Willoughbys and Crawfords; they add a sense of danger to the drawing-room which I was certain should be part of *Perfect Happiness*.

The sexual excitement felt in Austen novels comes from the attraction of personalities – a much more complicated and interesting source than the length of leg or size of bosom. This was the cue for me when writing about married love. I must hint at sexual frustration or the opposite by describing patterns of behaviour, strive for the subtlety of the indirect approach. In the end I was drawn slightly further into the bedroom than might have won Jane Austen's approval. But, if ever I felt moved to go even further, I remembered the passionate feelings aroused across the world by Darcy when – in an invention of the BBC television adaptation – he did no more than take off his coat, jump into a lake and re-emerge with his shirt clinging to his torso. A little overt action goes a long way when seen in the context of a society as formal and bound by manners and conventions as Jane Austen's.

Writing *Perfect Happiness* eight hours a day, seven days a week, I felt very close to Jane Austen and thought to myself that anyone wanting to understand her novels – literary critic, student or admiring reader – should try creating a chapter or two for themselves. Art students, after all, sit for hours copying Leonardos or Rembrandts, all the better to understand their style, even if they end up painting like Francis Bacon.

Indeed, one of the joys of writing *Perfect Happiness* has been the need to emulate the style of the master – complete with dashes, semi-colons and the wonderful balance of her sentences, in which the first half builds up for the second half to knock down: 'Mr Frank Churchill was one of the boasts of Highbury, and a lively curiosity to see him prevailed, though the compliment was so little returned that he had never been there in his life'.

Now that I have returned to my own work, I am dismally aware of the paucity of vocabulary in modern use and the sterile structure of much of our written language. Jane Austen, writing on the cusp of eighteenth-century elegance and nineteenth-century romanticism, perhaps had the best of both worlds. It is to our benefit that she also had an unsurpassed imagination and comic invention.

To the question I am continually asked: why is Jane Austen so popular at the moment, the honest answer is simple – because more people know about her. She has always been entertaining, instructive on human nature and on the nature of society but she was relegated, as great classics often are, to the schoolroom shelf. Her wider popularity is the greatest service film, television, radio, audiotape and sequel have achieved.

Lionel Blue
Rabbi and broadcaster

❦

I read Jane Austen because:
1. Her characters have both feet on the ground and she even tells you how much they earn and where their money is invested.
2. God comes to me through people-watching, as I think He came to her. She watched them in the drawing-room. I watch them on the concourse of a London station – but wherever, the same human comedy is played out.
3. If you didn't look at the human comedy with affection and compassion, you would burst into tears or go mad. She never actually says this but she must have thought and felt it.
4. She does not enthuse about religion or even say much about it but what she does say is true and free from falsehood or 'schmaltz'.

This is why I take her on holiday with me and re-read her frequently.

Elizabeth Bowen
novelist

❧

The constraints of polite behaviour only serve to store up her characters' energies; she dispels, except for the very stupid, the fallacy that life with the lid off – in thieves' kitchens, prisons, taverns and brothels – is necessarily more interesting than life with the lid on.

English Novelists, 1945

Humphrey Carpenter
biographer and journalist

❦

My happiest memories of holiday reading come from nearly 30 years ago, when I was about to get married, and we read the whole of Jane Austen aloud. It can't have taken long because, when we reached the end, we started all over again. It was a life-saver whenever we got stuck somewhere on holiday; I remember an entire morning in a remote railway junction in Normandy during a train strike, reading *Mansfield Park*, thanks to which the time passed incredibly swiftly and unstressfully. I haven't read Austen since those days; now, I think I would start with her last novel, *Persuasion*, which has an elegiac, autumnal tone, maybe more suitable for fiftysomethings like myself than the earlier, more high-spirited narratives.

From a *Sunday Times* feature on holiday reading, 27 June 1999

Tom Carpenter

Trustee and administrator,
the Jane Austen House Museum

❧

My first recollections of Jane Austen's House were around the age of 11 or 12 being brought down by my grandfather, Mr T. Edward Carpenter, and grandmother for the AGM day. At that time my grandfather was enjoying active retirement, having set up the Jane Austen Memorial Trust in 1949 and he visited the house one day a week handling all the administration from there and from his own home in Mill Hill, north-west London. It was indeed a fascinating hobby for him, giving many hours of pleasure and a world-wide correspondence. At that stage, apart from having seen and been much amused by the 1940 film of *Pride and Prejudice*, with Lawrence Olivier and Greer Garson, I have to confess that Jane Austen was not having a particularly strong impact on a boy who had the good fortune to have a father with an absorbing interest in model railways and railway history to occupy what might otherwise have been 'idle hours' – or more importantly, keeping me out of mischief. As it happened Jane Austen was not on my particular English literature prescribed reading list for my year of 'O' level, and apart from reading *Mansfield Park* round the family on holiday (away up in the Highlands of Scotland), her novels had largely passed over my head by the time I left school.

An active legal professional life, coupled with many hours spent as a Territorial Army soldier, meant there was little scope for leisure reading time, but I began to accompany my grandfather more frequently on his visits at other times in the year and to help with some of the basic administration of running the Trust through the facilities of our own legal business office in north London. After my grandfather died in 1969, effectively that administration devolved entirely on the shoulders of my late father, my brother and myself, with two other co-trustees (who at that time were Sir Hugh Smiley and Miss E. Jenkins), and the accounting and related paperwork generally came down to my department.

In 1994 a change in our practice arrangements had left me with more time in hand and Jean Bowden, our excellent curator, was hoping for some partial retirement. In September 1994, therefore, she handed over to me the remaining local administration work, whilst staying on as our archivist with all her expert knowledge in that field, and I came down for the first time to stay at Jane Austen's house itself. I will confess to some hasty catching up on her other novels, but perhaps as importantly, on absorbing the details of her own life and family. There is, in my view, certainly an advantage in coming to Jane Austen slightly later for some such as myself, because she certainly opens an amusing and fascinating aspect on history through her highly accurate reflection of the social situation of her own time.

As many will know, Jane Austen's House is rather box-like, rectangular and plain in its architectural style, for it was only ever intended to be a modest yeoman farmer's accommodation, let with the land it served. Yet to visitors far and wide it has an immediate welcoming ambience, pervaded by a calm, unhurried pace of life, a feeling which we otherwise miss today. It is easy to see why Jane at once became attached to it as her real home in those last crucial eight years of her life, and how that ambience and atmosphere enabled her writing talent to flourish. There is a homeliness about the creak of the floor-boards which unfailingly reminds you of where you are whenever you are moving about the house, yet the structure does not shake or move in bad or stormy weather even though it is timber framed, and there are none of those really surprising or mysterious creaks or groans which would suggest the existence of a ghost! Despite the huge number of visitors it remains a remarkably forgiving and easy house to clean, and is no trouble to keep tidy. The endless supply of fresh flowers is kept up by our assistant Administrator, Ann Channon, efforts which are rewardingly much remarked upon.

As a result of the conservation overhaul programme during the past eighteen years, every part of the house has now been checked and repairs are contained to routine preventive maintenance. In the garden, which is always available for people to enjoy whether the house is open or not, there are raspberries and gooseberries and we have reintroduced the vegetable patch to include runner beans, lettuces and other vegetables that surely the Austens themselves would have grown for their own consumption and sustenance. Every part of the buildings and outbuildings is now a hardworking element of the museum and visitor experience; with the service accommodation for the person tasked with the security presence on the first floor of the return wing above the Austens' former kitchen making a three-roomed flatlet.

You never know who will call by next! Her characters such as Mr Darcy and Miss Elizabeth Bennet (Colin Firth, Jennifer Ehle), Captain Wentworth and Anne Elliot (Ciaran Hinds and Amanda Root) spending a day here; well-known television presenters for filming like Sue Saville (GMTV), Liz McKean (BBC Breakfast News), Sally Taylor and Bruce Parker (BBC South), and the late Jill Dando (the Holiday programme) – all usually try out the

21

writing table in the dining parlour. And family are, of course, always especially welcome – the nine-year-old the other day who cautiously announced that she was Jane Austen's great, great ...great niece; and we checked, for she was indeed an eighth generation descendant from James Austen through Anna Lefroy.

I am very lucky to be on site for the duration of my task and I am thoroughly enjoying it. I just hope, for Jane Austen's own sake, that my explanations of what we think happened are reasonably accurate and a fair portrayal of what led to her great achievements.

Barbara Cartland

romantic novelist

♥

Jane Austen's works have given me many hours of plea-sure. And her books are a marvellous example of love and manners in polite society.

Years ago it was considered a great compliment for a man to be known as a 'perfect English gentleman' and we were known round the world for our good manners.

I think we should celebrate the millennium by bringing back good manners. It costs nothing for every man, woman and child to be polite and kind to those around them.

Sir Hugh Casson

architect, President of the Royal Academy 1976–84

❦

This was written by Sir Hugh Casson's daughter, Carola Zogolovitch, shortly before his death.

I am not sure how my father would have responded to your request but I do remember many visits to Chawton when we were children during the early fifties. We used to holiday down on the coast at Beaulieu and I think that it must have been a wet-weather outing. At any rate, it was our introduction to Jane Austen long before we read the books and it made a lasting impression on me. I particularly recall the dog cart in the stables and her desk in the sitting-room.

My father is a great Austen fan, probably as a result of his mother's love for her, and I am sure that had he been well enough he would have sent his own contribution.

Lord David Cecil

literary scholar

❧

Mere technical accomplishment is not enough to explain the impression she makes on us. After all, a work of art my be perfect technically and yet be a minor work, a porcelain vase, an ormolu snuff-box. And Jane Austen, so far from being a manufacturer of literary snuff-boxes, is one of the supreme novelists of the world. The absorbing, searching interest she awakes in the mind – so that one turns to her again and again and always finds something new to think about –is one only stirred by works of major art...

Jane Austen's range of character is very large. She painted on such a narrow canvas that people have not always realised this. But a wide canvas does not necessarily mean a wide range. Thackeray painted on a vast one, but his range of characters is small. For he always repeats them; his good women are all pictures of the same person in a different dress. Jane Austen's good women, Anne Elliot, Elinor Dashwood, Fanny Price, are all different. In her books she never repeats a single character. The snobbishness of the Rev. Mr Collins is unlike that of the Rev. Mr Elton: Isabella Thorpe and Lucy Steele are both calculating flirts but not the same sort of calculating flirt: there is all the difference in the world between the vulgarity of Mrs Bennet and the vulgarity of Mrs Jennings. Out of her small parsonage house Jane Austen's gay wand conjures innumerable troops of unique individuals.

So comprehensive and so searching a view of human nature inevitably invests her achievement with a universal character. For all that she paints the nineteenth century English scene with so sedulous an accuracy, this accuracy is an unimportant part of the impression she makes. *Mansfield Park* does not, like *Cranford*, appeal to us first of all by its period charm...

The unique irresistible flavour of her work, its gay astringent buoyancy, its silvery commonsense arises from the unexpected combination of her realistic moralism with the delicate elegance of its setting. Moreover, the fact that she kept so carefully to the only world she knew thoroughly well, meant that she was not distracted by superficial idiosyncrasies, but could penetrate beneath them to perceive its more general significance. *Emma* is universal just because it is narrow; because it confines itself to the range of Jane Austen's profoundest vision.

For it is a profound vision. There are other views of life and more extensive; concerned as it is exclusively with personal relationships, it leaves out several important aspects of experience. But on her own ground Jane Austen gets to the heart of the matter; her graceful unpretentious philosophy, founded as it is on unwavering recognition of fact, directed by an unerring perception of moral quality, is as impressive as those of the most majestic novelists. Myself I find it more impressive. If I were in doubt as to the wisdom of one of my actions I should not consult Flaubert or Dostoievsky. The opinion of Balzac or Dickens would carry little weight with me: were Stendhal to rebuke me, it would only convince me I had done right: even in the judgement of Tolstoy I should not put complete confidence. But I should be seriously upset, I should worry for weeks and weeks, if I incurred the disapproval of Jane Austen.

Poets and Story-tellers, 1949

Bruce Chatwin

travel writer

❧

Jane Austen was a comedian; her outlook was always humorous. And even when she penetrates into one of her characters with knife-edged clearness, she always does so with a smile on her lips.

From a Lower Sixth essay on *Pride and Prejudice*, quoted by Nicholas Shakespeare, in *Bruce Chatwin*, 1999

G.K. Chesterton
essayist

❧

Jane Austen was born before those bonds which (we are told) protected women from truth, were burst by the Brontës or elaborately untied by George Eliot. Yet the fact remains that Jane Austen knew much more about men than either of them. Jane Austen may have been protected from truth: but it was precious little of truth that was protected from her. When Darcy, in finally confessing his faults, says, 'I have been a selfish being all my life, in practice though not in theory,' he gets nearer to a complete confession of the intelligent male than ever was hinted at by the Byronic lapses of the Brontës' heroes or the elaborate exculpations of George Eliot's. Jane Austen, of course, covered an infinitely smaller field than any of her later rivals; but I have always believed in the victory of small nationalities.

The Victorian Age in Literature, 1913

Sir Winston Churchill

statesman (Prime Minister 1940–45, 1951–55)

❦

I decided to read a novel.[1] I had long ago read Jane Austen's *Sense and Sensibility*, and now I thought I would have *Pride and Prejudice*. Sarah[2] read it to me beautifully from the foot of the bed. I had always thought it would be better than its rival. What calm lives they had, those people! No worries about the French Revolution, or the crashing struggle of the Napoleonic wars. Only manners controlling natural passion as far as they could, together with cultural explanations of any mischances. All this seemed to go very well with M and B.[3]

The Second World War, 1952

1   While he was suffering from pneumonia at the height of the war
2   His eldest daughter
3   An early antibiotic (May and Baker)

Sebastian Coe
athlete and Member of Parliament

❧

As someone who has always been surrounded by and influenced by women with strong characters – particularly my wife who is the most influential person in my life – I have much affection for the characters in Jane Austen's novels.

Ivy Compton-Burnett
novelist

❧

I have read Jane Austen so much, and with such enjoyment
and admiration, that I may have absorbed things from her
unconsciously. I do not think myself that my books have
any real likeness to hers. I think that there is possibly some
likeness between our minds.

I. Compton-Burnett and M. Jourdain, 'A Conversation', *Orion*, 1944

Once I thought I should go mad because I couldn't finish
The Watsons.

Quoted by Hilary Spurling in *Secrets of a Woman's Heart: The Later Life
of I. Compton-Burnett*

Andrew Davies

screenwriter

❦

In adapting *Emma* I was particularly taken by the notion
that England never had a revolution because enough of its
aristocracy and gentry were like Mr Knightley; and I was
particularly moved by the plight of Jane Fairfax, hopelessly
in thrall to a manipulative and heartless lover.

Margaret Drabble
novelist and critic

❦

At a first reading, most find [Mr Bennet] much more attractive and judge him less harshly than his wife. This was certainly my own first response on reading the novel in the 1950s, and indeed tended then to be the received opinion. He is genuinely witty and intelligent: his sardonic remarks seem a fitting commentary on the vacuity of much of the social life in which he is reluctantly obliged to engage, and his view that 'we live, but to make sport for our neighbours, and laugh at them in our turn' may seem close to that of his author, and therefore to be condoned by her. I recall my indignation when asked to reassess him as a father, and consider whether Austen herself did not find him wanting.

On rereading one sees that she does indeed imply criticism of his negligence as a father, and recognises that his eccentricities are a hindrance to the matrimonial prospects of his daughters. Nevertheless, she relishes his ironic wit and clearly enjoys wreaking through his voice a little irresponsible revenge on the bores and fools of the neighbourhood. Nineteenth-century critics tended to view him indulgently, as a 'recluse' and an 'eccentric'. And nobody, not even Austen herself, seems to question how he actually spends his time. One might legitimately wonder if there is not as much vacuity in Mr Bennet's life as in that of his wife.

This, of course, is very much a feminist, twentieth-century perspective, and one that would have been difficult to perceive from within the society so faithfully depicted. Recent studies, predictably, have begun to produce defences of the vulgar, impossibly stupid, uncultured, embarrassing Mrs Bennet. Of course, we may now say, she was desperate to marry off her daughters: this was the 'employment' of her life, and she attacks it much more energetically than her husband does. She understands about dinners and balls and good cooking. We may wince from her pushiness and ignorance on first reading, but on the tenth are we not a little more impressed by the evidence that she runs a generous household, keeps a good table, is a good hostess?

Introduction to *Pride and Prejudice*, 1989

Ronald Duncan
playwright

❦

While we were rehearsing *Lucretia*[1] John Christie[2] invited Ben and me to write a new opera which he promised to present the following year. Ben agreed and said he wanted to write a comedy… During *Lucretia* rehearsals Ben had decided he wanted to write a work for Kathleen Ferrier.[3]

It was Joan Cross[4] who eventually produced a subject for us by suggesting *Mansfield Park*. She went off to Brighton especially to buy me a copy of the novel so that I could re-read it. As usual Ben was excited by the idea especially because the story was suitable for Kathleen, with a good part for Joan too. They were both anxious to get Jane Austen's elegant urbanity on to the operatic stage. Again we worked out a dramatic synopsis first and then broke this down into a musical synopsis: aria, duet, recitative etc. When this was completed I began to write the libretto. We had settled on the title *Letters to William*. The Christies were delighted, mainly because Ben had said there would be a part for Audrey's pug.[5]

Working with Britten: A Personal Memoir, 1981

1 Duncan was the librettist of Benjamin Britten's opera *The Rape of Lucretia*, first performed at Glyndebourne in 1946
2 John Christie founded Glyndebourne Festival Opera for his wife, the soprano Audrey Mildmay
3 Kathleen Ferrier, the contralto, created the role of Lucretia
4 Joan Cross created the role of the Female Chorus in *Lucretia*
5 Though Duncan wrote part of the libretto for the *Mansfield Park* opera, Britten abandoned the project.

Ranulph Fiennes
explorer

❦

I have Jane Austen as my distinguished forebear and I'm especially happy to have a touch of her blood as I love her works. Her humour is well exampled in one of her letters to her sister: 'The doctor was in such deep mourning that either his mother, his wife or himself must be dead'.

Rachael Heyhoe Flint

sportswoman

❦

Having spent all my life running around on 'sports fields various', the literary experiences of my life have been some-what fleeting, to say the least.

I do however vividly remember having to study *Pride and Prejudice* as one of our novels for 'O' level English Literature. I loved this book more than any other of the required reading – probably because I could understand and appreciate its content more comfortably than any of the others! Good plain English, colourful descriptions and a fun story line.

E.M. Forster
novelist

❦

Why do the characters in Jane Austen give us a slightly new pleasure each time they come in, as opposed to the merely repetitive pleasure that is caused by a character in Dickens? The answer to this question can be put several ways: that unlike Dickens, she was a real artist, that she never stooped to caricature, etc. But the best reply is that her characters though smaller than his are more highly organised. They function all round, and even if her plot made greater demands on them than it does, they would still be adequate. Suppose that Louisa Musgrove had broken her neck on the Cobb. The description of her death would have been feeble and ladylike – physical violence is quite beyond Miss Austen's powers – but the survivors would have reacted properly as soon as the corpse was carried away, they would have brought into view new sides of their characters, and though *Persuasion* would have been spoiled as a book, we should know more than we do about Captain Wentworth and Anne. All the Jane Austen characters are ready for an extended life, for a life which the scheme of her books seldom requires them to lead, and that is why they lead their actual lives so satisfactorily.

Aspects of the Novel, 1927

Margaret Forster
novelist and biographer

❦

I don't think I have much to say about Jane Austen – not, alas, a favourite of mine. First read her at seven, starting with 'A's' in the adult library, and found her so dull. Passed on to 'B's' and was much happier with the Brontës. Did *Pride and Prejudice* for 'O' level and still hated her – but then, around 40, reading her to review something for television or film, suddenly did start to recognise and appreciate her wit and irony, though admiration still doesn't make me really love her.

John Fowles

novelist, resident of Lyme Regis

Jane Austen's connections with Lyme are well known, though in one way they were short. We recently had fresh reason to admire them in Mike Healy's adaptation of *Persuasion*, always one of my favourites among her novels. I had the pleasure of taking Mike round Lyme. It is not really for me to judge on how successfully he conveyed this town (or as it was nearly two centuries ago) with the text of her book.

I am perhaps somewhat peculiar in preferring a writer who, though her contemporary, has for long been seen as someone condemned to live in her shadow: that is Thomas Love Peacock; but in a way, and perhaps especially with *Persuasion*, I think Jane's virtues are especially clear and relevant. Partly, Lyme was made to fit her, to suit her, but her excellence seems to me unmistakably in her setting of the moral values. There she felt right – indeed I think I would cite right feeling as her true genius. We see it in her sometimes tart wit or her somehow always rather naval sentimentality.

Jane is indeed never quite credible in her moral richness. She almost constitutes a separate human drive or characteristic of psychology. Jane is almost unique in her ability to express something most of us know, yet leave out of the ordinary picture of our race. We have no name for her quasi-divine probity, her summoning and evocation of so many desirable social and racial values.

We are currently here in Lyme trying to rejuvenate an

old theatre. It seems to me there is only one name with which we might, indeed ought, to baptize it: Jane Austen.

Stella Gibbons

novelist

❦

Whenever a reader thinks of those passionate, suffering creatures, Emily Brontë, Emily Dickinson, Christina Rossetti, and wonders, a little despondently perhaps, whether happiness must be sacrificed by women artists to produce good work, this same reader can open her *Persuasion* with a contented little sigh, remembering that at least one woman artist, and one of the most exquisite, enjoyed life, flirted, and dearly loved her sister.

Quoted by Reggie Oliver in *Out of the Woodshed: a Portrait of Stella Gibbons*, 1998

There is no poetry in her writing, nor any mystery beyond that of plot, nor is there any religious feeling; there are no gulfs and no heights.

Introduction to a American edition of *Sense and Sensibility*, 1957

Rupert Hart-Davis
publisher and writer

❦

I'm with you about Jane Austen,[1] who has never been a great favourite of mine. But it's so long since I read her (except for one, of which more in a minute) that I'd like to try again with the cold eye of middle age before finally jumping down on your side of the fence. I see what so many other people see in her, but myself (tell it not in Bloomsbury) if I want to refresh myself in that period I prefer Scott. My uncle Duff[2] adored her novels, and in the last week of his life, when he knew (consciously or subconsciously) that he hadn't long to live, he came to Soho Square on Christmas Eve, and, saying 'I've brought you a Christmas present: I hope you haven't got it already,' he pulled two slim volumes out of each pocket of his greatcoat. They were the first edition of *Northanger Abbey* and *Persuasion* (4 vols), in which he had written 'Old men forget but they are grateful when they remember'. I was much touched at the time, and when he died suddenly at sea on New Year's Day, the books became doubly precious, as his farewell gift. Later that year (1954), still moved by the same emotion, I re-read *Persuasion* in this copy, and persuaded myself (almost) that I shared Duff's admiration for it. But in truth I don't think I did. When, oh when, shall I have the leisure to try the others again and report fully to you?

From a letter to George Lyttleton, 24 February 1957

1. See p.p 58–9
2. Duff Cooper, British diplomat

John Dixon Hunt
literary scholar and garden historian

🍎

It's a famous passage in *Emma*: 'It was a sweet view – sweet to the eye and to the mind. English verdure, English culture, English comfort, seen under a sun bright, without being oppressive.' Many who pause at this moment during the visit to Donwell Abbey, when Emma begins to appreciate her possible place in society, will cherish its celebration of the English landscape and will acknowledge its wondering, if (perhaps) slightly ironic, applause of patriotic topophilia.

But Emma's moment of revelation is also one of the shrewdest pieces of commentary on the phenomenon known as the English landscape garden. Its shrewdness is all the more admirable if we think of the climate of landscape taste in which it was made in 1816.

What Emma both sees and intuits is a landscape that has been deliberately designed and culturally manipulated as an expression of Englishness. Contrary to the prevailing naturalism of garden theory at the time, she recognizes in the Donwell Abbey landscape a contrived epitome of country and nation.

The prevalent naturalism had been fostered by Horace Walpole and Thomas Whately, the two able and influential proponents of the 'natural', 'modern' or 'English' garden. For Walpole, writing in the 1760s, this landscape style was a perfect perfection, an elimination of all the foreign artfulness that had plagued garden design from Babylon to Versailles and Hampton Court. True, he acknowledged the role of painters like William Kent in its creation (his *History of the Modern Taste in Gardening* had been published first as part of his *Anecdotes of Painting in England*), and it is one of Walpole's unresolved contradictions that he lauds naturalism contrived by a painter. But Walpole, like Whately in his *Observations on Modern Gardening* (1770), insisted above all on the return of garden design to its 'natural' state, which was indubitably English. A character in Tom Stoppard's *Arcadia*, who has probably read his/her Walpole, puts it nicely: 'Nature as God intended'!

But the objection to such claims is that if you eliminate the art from the landscape you won't recognise it as art any more. Sir Joshua Reynolds put it succinctly, even magisterially: 'Gardening, as far as gardening is an art, or entitled to that appellation, is a deviation from nature; for if the true taste consists, as many hold, in banishing every appearance of art, or any traces of the footsteps of man, it would then be no longer a garden.'

Emma's epiphany is not so professorial; nor is it wholly innocent of picturesque sensibility or acknowledgement of the 'appearance of art'. But she sees the landscape of the Donwell Abbey estate as an expression of Englishness, as a subtle but still calculated *version* of a natural scenery and society. It includes, we must assume, designed space as well as the agrarian land of Abbey Mill Farm; the first is deliberate art; the second the due process of cultural growth and intervention, but this last is given significance by its juxtaposition with the designed spaces. All 'nature' is a garden. The *ensemble* appeals as much to the mind as to the eye; it speaks of calculation, of art (both fine and social).

In the years since Walpole rewrote the history of gardens, we have all tended to slip into the error of thinking garden-making is a natural process. Recently, ecological imperatives, too, have reinforced this fallacy. The legacy of

45

Walpolean history-writing pervades explicitly or implic- itly (and so insidiously) most commentaries on place-making, whether it be as gardens or larger land- scapes like national parks. Emma's 'particular observation' and 'exact understanding' are a fine corrective, and we probably need an Emma-directed history of garden-making that sees them as an art of representation. That would address, especially, how the 'English' landscape was adapted to other verdures, other cultures and under brighter suns when it was translated to Europe and the United States.

P.D. James

novelist

❦

I first read Jane Austen when I was eight or nine years old and attended the Sunday School attached to Ludford church. There was a small cupboard in the hall with a number of books which we children could borrow. Some, like *The Wide, Wide World, A Peep Behind the Scenes* and *Jessica's First Prayer* were of depressing piety, but I also discovered there *Little Women* and *Pride and Prejudice*. It seems curious now that the latter should appeal to a child so young, but I was hungry for books and this was one I could both read and to an extent understand, although the irony must have eluded me. Jane Austen has remained my favourite author.

It seems extraordinary, if it is indeed true, that she was once seen as a gently-born, pure-minded spinster, dutiful daughter, compliant sister, affectionate aunt. We don't need the letters to show us a different Jane. There is passion in the novels, even if it is too subtle to be recognized by Charlotte Brontë. And there is passion, too, in her life, if only the passion of what the critic D.W. Harding described as 'regulated hatred'. To me it is far more like controlled resentment. We have to resist the temptation to foist on to her a twentieth-century sensibility; she was hardly deprived by domesticity of a university education or a profession, but she must have known that, however brilliant or successful her brothers, it was she who had genius. And yet, until she could earn from her novels, she was without power to control her own life. If her father decided to move to Bath, then Jane moved, neither consulted nor considered. Every penny she had to spend came from her father or a brother. Even Cassandra had the income from the £1,000 left to her by her fiancé. Jane had nothing. No wonder she said, once the money started coming in, that it was the pewter as well as the fame that she relished.

From *Time to be in Earnest: a fragment of autobiography*, 1999

Selma James
author and critic

❧

Virginia Woolf compared Jane Austen to Shakespeare. After years of reading and re-reading Austen novels late at night to replenish my fighting spirit, I agree that it is a fair comparison. Virginia Woolf claims that Ms Austen's sentence is female. There I am on shakier ground because I am not a creator of fiction and cannot hear a literary cadence as she did. But I do know that Jane Austen speaks for me, not only because she says things I want said, or because she says things I need to hear, but also because she is always saying so many things at once, much as we women perceive a thousand truths even in chance conversation – so many we don't know how many. Who else has done that for us? Very few. And Ms Austen did it first. She broke the ground and, though she is loved, her work is often trivialised for doing it.

The Ladies and the Mammies, 1983

Paul Johnson
journalist

❦

Jane Austen's handbag, I imagine, would be worth a book in itself: very large but not at all grungy, and fitted out to utilitarian principles (she was a contemporary of Jeremy Bentham) with everything that might be needed by a lady with a passionate interest in clothes forced by circumstances to make her own. Thus, she would have India tape, scraps of jute webbing, piping cord, press-studs, needles galore (and needle-threaders in later life), ric-rac, seam-binding, markers and mending wool, thread snips, thimbles, twist-pins, curlifil, bodkins and bump interlining, a darning mushroom, slivers of Hessian and Russian braid, Guterman threads and Offray ribbons, slipping-thread, silesia and small squares of felt. Plenty of bobbins, too, dressmaker's pins, Bolton twill, beeswax, scrim and gimp-braids, and maybe Cassandra's latest letter crowning the whole.

From *The Spectator*, 27 November 1999

David Kossoff
actor, writer and broadcaster

❦

A marvellous observer, with a calm gaze, missing nothing.
Innate good manners. What a dinner-party companion!
She would sit, listen, make no impolite comment at the daft
remark, the idiotic generalisation, the racist, the show-off.
If she had accepted me as congenial, on her private wave-
length, I would receive a side-long glance, a murmured
word, a smile (well-bred but with mischief in it). We would
both know she was making notes in the mind, to be used
later. Everything would be used; what people left *unsaid*,
too. She would eat and drink with great delicacy. She would
be a delight to me. If I told her I was working on a book,
she would show real interest, but would with courtesy
show me when to stop going on about it. Bless her. She has
enriched us.

Philip Larkin

poet

❦

The only feature of the day I am sorry about is your decision about Barbara Pym.[1] I am not very good at expressing my thoughts on the spur of the moment, but in retrospect what I feel is this: by all means turn it down if you think it's a bad book of its kind, but please don't turn it down because it's the kind of book it is... I feel it is a great shame if ordinary sane novels about ordinary sane people doing ordinary sane things can't find a publisher these days. This is in the tradition of Jane Austen & Trollope, and I refuse to believe that no one wants its successors today.

Letter to Charles Montieth, 15 August 1965

I must say I'd rather read a new B.P. than a new J.A.!

Letter to Barbara Pym, 22 March 1972

1. Faber and Faber had declined to publish *An Unsuitable Attachment*, eventually published posthumously by Macmillan in 1982.

D.H. Lawrence

novelist and poet

❦

Dear Mrs Jackson,

I must tell you I am in the middle of reading your novel. You have very often a simply *beastly* style, indirect and roundabout and stiff-kneed and stupid. And your stuff is abominably muddled – you'll simply have to write it all again. But it is fascinatingly interesting. Nearly all of it is *marvellously* good. It is only so incoherent. But you can *easily* pull it together. It *must* be a long novel – it is of the quality of a long novel. My stars, just you work at it, and you'll have a piece of work you never need feel ashamed of...

When I've finished it – tomorrow or Wednesday – we must have a great discussion about it. My good heart, there's some honest work here, real.

I must go to Croydon tomorrow afternoon. But I'll ring you up when I've finished.

Yours,

D.H. Lawrence

You must be willing to put much real work, hard work, into this, and you'll have a genuine creative piece of work. It's like Jane Austen at a deeper level.

Letter to Catherine Carswell, July 1914

F.R. Leavis
literary critic

❦

The possible uses of literature to the historian and sociologist are many in kind, and all the important ones demand that the user shall be able, in the fullest sense, to read. If, for instance, we want to go further than the mere constatation that a century and a half ago the family counted for much more than it does now, if we want some notion of the difference involved in day-to-day living – in the sense of life and its dimensions and in its emotional and moral accenting – for the ordinary cultivated person, we may profitably start trying to form it from the novels of Jane Austen. But only if we are capable of appreciating shade, tone, implication and essential structure – as (it is necessary to add) none of the academically, or fashionably, accredited authorities seems to be.

The Common Pursuit, 1952

David Lodge
novelist and literary critic

❦

These boo-words, 'insular', 'parochial' and 'domestic' could be used against Jane Austen – and have been used on occasions. But she was a great writer. It is easy to mistake what is exotic and unfamiliar for real originality.

From *The Guardian*, 11 May 1999, commenting on the Orange Prize short-list controversy

Elizabeth Longford
historian and biographer

❧

The happy hours I spent reading Jane Austen's novels went through two distinct stages, separated from each other by at least forty years. During the first stage, I was a young student of literature reading Jane Austen with sheer delight and analysing the reasons for my pleasure only when absolutely forced to stop and do so. I knew some of the answers, involving her brilliant sense of humour, her characterisation and so on, but one of the main reasons for her unique success had hitherto eluded me. Then something happened that made it seem likely I would never discover one of the most interesting causes of Jane Austen's triumph in the literary world. I stopped reading English at Oxford and changed over to reading *Literae Humanores* – History and Philosophy in the original Greek and Latin. Jane was elbowed out by Thucydides and Tacitus.

It began like this. Ancient History led me on to a passion for the problems of modern English and European history. By the late 1960s I was engaged on writing a two-volume life of the Duke of Wellington and my mind was running on the Napoleonic Wars. What did it feel like to be living in England during those hectic days?

I had known the Kent and Sussex coast since childhood, with its guardian castles and Martello towers. Now I was staying at Stratfield Saye, the victor of Waterloo's country home, and the then Duke of Wellington had taken me over to Jane Austen's home nearby for an enthusiastic visit and lecture. Suddenly I realised the name of the person who would tell me what it was like to live in the England of Wellington and Napoleon. Jane Austen. I rushed to my row of small red leather books again, with their elegant gilt titles and pretty illustrations, and settled down to re-entering England in the Napoleonic age under the infallible guidance of my new historical friend.

No such thing. As I read on, Wellington and Napoleon were far from seeming just round the corner. Of course there were soldiers and sailors around – where are there not? Of course Jane knew her Prince Regent (afterwards George IV) and indeed dedicated one of her novels to him. But the point was that with Jane Austen you did not enter the age of Wellington, or any other era great or small, for that matter. Her genius had been to create a world of her own that was entirely invented yet completely real, new yet ageless, familiar yet never actually to be met with. The ultimate charm of Jane Austen had been discovered at last. She had created the Jane Austen world for us of the modern age to revel in. So I started re-reading her in a new spirit. And as the years passed by it seemed quite right and natural that others – my friend Emma Tennant and my daughter Rachel Billington – should introduce us to satellites from that Janeite world known as 'sequels'.

George Lyttleton
Eton schoolmaster

❦

I *will not* be bullied into reading Jane Austen over and over again, as the David Cecils and others say one ought to and they do. And I *will* say with my last breath that Miss Bates in *Emma* is a *shattering* bore, Mr Knightley only just not a tremendous prig, and Emma herself vain, conceited, and unamusing – and indeed crying aloud for smacks on that area of her person which no doubt she would rather have died than allude to.

From a letter to Rupert Hart-Davis, 8 March 1956

I am humbly but testily re-reading *Emma.* You always deride my habit of re-reading stuff to which I have been allergic, and I think it is fairly absurd. But so many good men and so many too many even better women do go on so about the woman Austen – and as Tolstoy said about lovers of Shakespeare, I can only conclude that the 'Janeites' are all mad. I am half-way through, and send you an interim report, viz that the conversations in the book fall mainly under two heads, i.e. Mrs Dale,[1] and passages

1. *Mrs Dale's Diary* was a long-running radio serial

to be put into Latin Prose. Mr Woodhouse ('Oh my dear, *deliciously* amusing!') hits exactly the same note every time he comes in, and the boringness of Miss Bates is positively overwhelming. No more o' that i' God's name.

From a letter to Rupert Hart-Davis, 10 September 1958

Harold Macmillan

statesman (Prime Minister 1957–63)

❦

[On 9 January 1957] the Queen's acceptance of her Prime Minister's[1] resignation was announced. The next morning I thought it wiser not to go to the Treasury. I heard that Lord Salisbury and Sir Winston Churchill had been sent for by the Queen. But since no one had told me about what had taken place the night before, I had no idea of what advice they would give... I passed the morning in the downstairs sitting-room [of 11 Downing Street], to which I had restored the picture of Mr Gladstone, and I read *Pride and Prejudice* – very soothing. At noon Sir Michael Adeane[2] rang up and asked me to be at the Palace at 2 o'clock. So it was settled.

Riding the Storm: 1956–1959, 1971

---

1   Anthony Eden
2   The Queen's Private Secretary

Katherine Mansfield
short story writer

❦

She makes modern episodic people like me, as far as I go,
look very incompetent ninnies.

Letter to Elizabeth, Countess Russell, December 1921

W. Somerset Maugham
novelist

❧

Jane Austen's novels are pure entertainment. If you happen to believe that to entertain should be the novelist's main endeavour, you must put her in a class by herself. Greater novels than hers have been written, *War and Peace*, for example, and the *Brothers Karamazov*; but you must be fresh and alert to read them with profit. No matter if you are tired and dispirited, Jane Austen's enchant.

Ten Novels and Their Authors, 1954

Ellen Moers
literary critic

❦

In the work of Jane Austen, the author eludes us: that is
one of the reasons many have coupled her name with
Shakespeare's when saluting Austen's rare quality. But
where with Shakespeare we are still searching for clues to
his occupations, travels and acquaintances, with Jane
Austen we know quite enough about her life to satisfy our
curiosity about her non-literary, non-domestic activities
with a single word: none. Instead, our curiosity is all about
Austen's temper and mind. When did she laugh, and when
grow serious? What did she hold as a moralist? Where did
she stand – we want the answer almost in a physical sense
– in relation to her characters? It is very difficult to know.

For example, near the end of *Emma*, Mrs Weston has a
baby that turns out to be a girl. Mrs Weston, the heroine's
genteel and now well-married former governess, remains
a friend and neighbor to Emma, who rejoices in the sex of
the child, for Emma is 'convinced that a daughter would
suit both father and mother best. It would be a great
comfort to Mr Weston as he grew older … to have his fire-
side enlivened by the sports and nonsense, the freaks and
the fancies of a child never banished from home'. Good God!
Was Jane Austen so little a feminist that she did not protest
her own lifelong imprisonment at home? Is she with Emma
here or against her, as her heroine takes the paternalistic
view of the spinster daughter's doom? Impossible to know.

Literary Women, 1978

Vladimir Nabokov

novelist

❦

At first sight Jane Austen's manner and matter may seem to be old-fashioned, stilted, unreal. But this is a delusion to which the bad reader succumbs. The good reader is aware that the quest for real life, real people, and so forth is a meaningless process when speaking of books... There is no such thing as real life for an author of genius: he must create it himself and then create the consequences. The charm of *Mansfield Park* can be fully enjoyed only when we adopt its conventions, its rules, its enchanting make-believe. Mansfield Park never existed, and its people never lived.

Miss Austen's is not a violently vivid masterpiece as some other novels in this series are. Novels like *Madame Bovary* or *Anna Karenin* are delightful explosions admirably controlled. *Mansfield Park*, on the other hand, is the work of a lady and the game of a child. But from that workbasket comes exquisite needlework art, and there is a streak of marvellous genius in that child.

Lectures on Literature, 1980

Nigel Nicolson
writer and publisher

❦

It was in gratitude to the Regency period, which gave us some of our loveliest architecture and landscapes, that I returned after many years to Jane Austen. Like many exiles, I read her novels during the war, telling myself that her idealised version of England was what we were fighting for. It was also the period of urban poverty, Botany Bay, cholera and satanic mills, but it is undeniable that England before the trains and trams, the tractor and bus, looked its most serene. It was still largely rural, and in small towns like Guildford and Alton the neatness of the houses and dignity of the municipal buildings expressed a universal taste that we lost somewhere about 1830. Before then our forebears could not fashion a cottage chair or a pewter coffee-pot without creating an object of utility and grace, and these things were taken so much for granted in Jane Austen's day that she never expresses any pleasure in them, or surprise. It is strange that to her, a vicar's daughter, a parish church was simply the place where you go to be married in the last chapter, not a place of worship or historical and aesthetic interest, and the beautiful country houses where she danced and sometimes stayed were just settings for the small conflicts between generations and classes, and the little moves that young people made, and still make, towards or away from each other, that she depicts so precisely in her books.

I wanted to discover more about the places she knew and how she used them in her novels. It would be a pleasant way of passing a summer. So in 1990 I drove round southern England with my photographer, Stephen Colover, and together we compiled the book which was published the following year under the title *The World of Jane Austen.*

Her birthplace, Steventon Rectory in Hampshire, where she spent the first twenty-five years of her short life, was pulled down soon after her death, but Chawton Cottage, near Alton, survives as her memorial. It was there that she revised her first three novels and wrote the last three, all in a period of seven years. It tells us little that we could not have gathered from her books and letters, except that she saw no need for a room of her own, sharing a tiny bedroom with her sister Cassandra and writing her novels on a little tripod table in the dining-room after the breakfast things had been cleared away.

She was a great walker, and I spent much of that summer tracing the paths that she had followed from village to village, farm to farm, which are easily identifiable from her letters. The more I studied her simple life, the more I liked her good nature, her inquisitiveness and humour. There is nothing in her letters to confirm the notion of a sour and unattractive spinster that we derive largely from Cassandra's unflattering watercolour sketch of her when Jane was aged about thirty-five. She and her siblings were much in demand as guests in the local country houses. My favourite Hampshire house is Ibthorpe near the border with Berkshire where she often stayed with the Lloyd family, and where, by coincidence, the painter Dora Carrington spent part of her childhood and youth, ignorant that Jane Austen had lived there too.

Long Life, 1997

Matthew Parris

journalist and political commentator

❦

The proliferation of plays, films and TV costume dramas based on Austen's novels worries me. They are often beautifully done and bring her stories to life in some measure. But what is so distinctive and refreshing to me about Austen as an author is the authorial *tone*. There is a caustic quality to her narrative – and narrative is inclined to be lost in stage and screen dramatisations. The author's voice loses its predominance when characters speak for themselves.

Someone once referred to the 'regulated hatred' that breathes through an Austen novel.[1] That goes too far, but the saccharine quality that creeps into costume drama falls short. We are left with too much prettiness, and of course the *plot* – the least important thing. A little more venom, ladies, please.

1. D.W. Harding, 'Regulated Hatred', *Scrutiny*, 1940

William Plomer

poet and author

❦

I'm much too easily put off a writer by the antics of his admirers. I love Jane Austen, but when her admirers call themselves 'Janeites' and begin smirking and making masonic grimaces at one another, whether in speech or in print, a blind spot rushes to my head, and I rush for consolation to some splendid but cultless old girl. In a case like that, Maria Edgeworth would do nicely.

'An Alphabet of Literary Prejudice', 1946

Beatrix Potter

children's writer

❦

I find the names of the streets rather melancholy here. Do
you remember Miss Austen's *Persuasion*, with all the scenes
and streets in Bath? It was always my favourite, and I read
the end part of it again last July. On the 26th, the day after
I got Norman's[1] letter, I thought my story had come right,
with patience and waiting, like Anne Elliot's did.

Letter to Millie Warne, 1905

1. Norman Warne, the recently deceased fiancé and publisher of Beatrix
Potter.

J.B. Priestley
novelist and playwright

❦

It says much for [Sir Walter Scott's] perception that he was among the first to recognise the supremacy of Jane Austen in her own kind of fiction, the domestic novel, which was also being written by Fanny Burney, Maria Edgeworth, Susan Ferrier, all three women of talent but well below the delicate art, the astonishing perfection, of Jane Austen, who has fascinated every succeeding generation of English readers. Her acute sense of character, her bland irony, her exquisite powers of organisation and presentation, turned the uneventful lives of well-fed people in quiet corners into enchanting novels.

Literature and Western Man, 1962

Barbara Pym
novelist

❦

Visit to Jane Austen's house with Bob. I put my hand down on Jane's desk and bring it up covered with dust. Oh that some of her genius might rub off on me! One would have imagined the devoted female custodian going round with her duster at least every other day. Then to the site of Steventon Rectory the place of her birth – now a field overgrown with nettles and docks. We went into Steventon Church – very cool inside. Steventon Manor is deserted and overgrown, not beautiful but sad, almost romantic. Such enormous beech trees and that *silence* – a few miles away the road from Basingstoke to London and the traffic roaring by.

Diary entry, 11 August 1969, quoted in *A Very Private Eye: an Autobiography in Letters and Diaries*, ed. Hazel Holt and Hilary Pym, 1984

John Rae

former Headmaster, Westminster School

🍐

I read *Pride and Prejudice* for the first time in my sixties and was astonished to find just how sharp, realistic and cynical Jane Austen was about human nature. I think I had expected some sort of comedy of manners that was witty and elegant but lacking in bite. I was delighted to discover that the novel was not a period piece. What Jane Austen writes about human motivation rings true at every turn.

It does not matter that her novels were written and re-written at a time when morals and manners were different from our own, we still experience the moments of recognition – 'yes, that's exactly how people think and act'. The popularity of the film and television adaptations owes everything to the 'truth' of her characters and of their relations with one another and nothing to the superficial attractions of costume drama.

Mary Robinson

United Nations High Commissioner and
former President of the Irish Republic

❧

Jane Austen passes the test of a truly great writer in that
her works can be read many times with pleasure. I first read
her novels when I was a student and happily re-read them;
but I confess I can be irritated by some television produc-
tions of her work!

Among her many qualities is the fact that she is a role
model for women writers. She excelled in a male-domi-
nated profession. The heroines she portrayed are
particularly striking, Emma Woodhouse, Elizabeth Bennet
and Anne Elliot being just three memorable examples.

It says a lot about Jane Austen's genius that her books
still appeal to new generations of readers. In spite of the
great changes that have taken place since she wrote, her
characters still speak to us; the choices and moral dilemmas
they face are still relevant. Above all, her sharp eye and
keen sense of humour retain the capacity to amuse and
instruct us 200 years later.

Dorothy L. Sayers

writer

❦

Glad you like Jane Austen, Tootles;[1] she's one of the people about whom there is no question at all. I read *Northanger Abbey* for the first time the other day, and Lord! it was good.

From a letter to her parents, 1918

I have no news, except that – looking forward to the confidently-expected food-crisis, I have purchased two hens. In their habits they display, respectively Sense and Sensibility, and I have therefore named them Elinor and Marianne. Elinor is a round, comfortable, motherly-looking little body, who lays one steady, regular, undistinguished egg per day, and allows nothing to disturb her equanimity (except, indeed, the coal-cart, to which both take exception). Marianne is leggier, timid, and liable to hysterics. Sometimes she lays a shell-less egg, sometimes a double yolk, sometimes no egg at all. On the days when she lays no egg she nevertheless goes and sits in the nest for the usual time, and seems to imagine that nothing more is required. As my gardener says: 'She just *thinks* she's laid an egg'. Too much imagination – in fact, Sensibility. But when she does lay an egg it is larger than Elinor's. But you cannot wish to listen to this cackle…

From a letter to C.S. Lewis, 2 June 1947

1. Her father, the Revd Henry Sayers

Brian Southam

Chairman of the Jane Austen Society

❦

We enter the new Millennium to discover that Jane Austen, far from breathless and lagging behind, has already taken a step into the twenty-first century. Posters for Richard Branson's Virgin Bookstore in New York ask insistently 'Do you swim in pop culture by day, but relax with Jane Austen at night? do you?' and an Internet search on www.altavista.com turns up nearly sixteen thousand website references. So there is no fear of her fading from view.

My personal celebration will be in setting aside a few days for reading the collected letters from end to end, to hear, as nearly as I can, the authentic voice in autobiographical mode, retailing the news of the day and the gossip of the neighbourhood, reporting her latest reading or the state of her writing or the cut of her dress, or advising nephews and nieces in Aunterly tones. I can then move on from that fountain of delight, a well-spring spirited to the very end, to that parallel universe of the novels themselves, a world Jane Austen was at liberty to populate and construct and reconstruct at will, a realm in which to explore all she loved and all she hated and all the irritations and annoyances that stand mid-way between, a freedom that we would all love to enjoy ourselves!

Freya Stark

traveller and writer

❦

I have read the whole of Jane Austen and think of beginning over again. What a perfect woman – not only a writer – and what a *sham* she makes all this female emancipation seem! Arabic is too *real* for it, nothing that is not genuine can stand this primitive severity. But Jane would have been quite at home and talked tea-table gossip with the ladies of Huraidha.

From a letter to her mother, 31 January 1938

I am reading Jane Austen (it was about ten years since last time) and it is as fresh and exciting as always. Emma is a bit of a prig but Mr Knightley is her best hero, and what a picture of the village! I am trying to think what gives this permanent freshness, and I believe that it is because with all her insuperable keenness she is not merely observant, she is interested in the meaning of the things she notes. I think that is the difference between her and the modern novelists who put the observations down without drawing final conclusions. Jane, you feel, thought the conclusion the most important part and that gets the whole picture into place and when the quiet little climax comes, Mr Knightley's few words, Mr Darcy's second proposal, there is a tremendous *meaning* packed into that simplicity. And

76

she is always right; never deceived by sentiment, but never undervaluing the reality behind it: her world is still the real world and always will be, and so brought down to essentials that, in spite of the different setting, one need never make allowances (as with Brontës or Eliot) for differences of place or time. The people are just what they would be if they lived now, because she is interested in the essential substance of them and her values are as permanent as those of Shakespeare or Homer. And what terseness: Mrs Norris, the vicar's widow, and the new vicar who 'were seldom good friends: their acquaintance had begun in dilapidations and their habits were totally dissimilar'. There it is: with nothing to be added.

From a letter to Stewart Perowne, 14 August 1952

Emma Thompson
actress and author of screenplay for
Sense and Sensibility

❧

It's really a disaster how writers like Shakespeare and Austen are taught in school. Everything that's good about them is somehow drained away because one is required to analyse them. They're so brilliant about human nature and so contemporary and yet, somehow, the study of them relegates them to some awful, dusty library with dead flies on the windows!

Quoted in 'Making sense of Austen's classic', *Toronto Sun*, 1995

You can't feminise Jane Austen because she was living before those ideas were current... But the point is you don't have to contemporise that, because she is contemporary – she describes universal characters and human behaviour and rites of passage.

Quoted in 'Sense of a woman', *Sunday Mail Magazine*, 25 February 1996

William Waldegrave

Cabinet minister 1990–97

❦

Gilbert Ryle, the philosopher, was alleged to have said that there was no reason to read anything other than Jane Austen, but you should read her all, every year. I do not quite go that far; but it is entirely true that the more I read her the more I admire her. So subtle is she that the pleasure of greeting an old and familiar friend is nearly always sharpened by the discovery of something new which, inexplicably, you have not noticed before. It is like listening to the Goldberg Variations, or reading (I hope Austenians will not be offended) P.G. Wodehouse. These are true desert island choices; they never stale, because beneath apparently limpid surfaces, immensely complicated things are happening, the unravelling of which you never fully complete.

Mary Warnock
philosopher

❧

Once when I was a teacher of philosophy in Oxford I was giving a tutorial to two girls, and our topic was 'truth in art'. They were reading for the school of Philosophy and Modern Languages, one studying German, the other French, so they had plenty of literary examples at their finger-tips, but in their essays both chose to take examples only from the visual arts. So, to broaden things out a bit, I offered them a scene from a novel, the picnic on Box Hill from *Emma*. I said I thought this was the most painfully true piece of writing I knew.

I need not, as I did not then, rehearse the story in all its detail; I reminded them only that Emma had been unable to resist making a joke at the good Miss Bates's expense. And then, the dreadful picnic over, there came Mr Knightley's reproach: "'Emma, I had not thought it possible'". And I reminded them how Emma had tried to laugh it off, and how Mr Knightley had left before she could express her remorse. 'Never had she felt so agitated, mortified, grieved, at any circumstance in her life… she felt it at the heart.' And the tears ran down her face all the way home.

My pupils looked at me pityingly as I reminded them of Emma's agony. 'Is that not a totally true account?' I asked. One of them said, in astonishment, 'I believe you identify yourself with Emma.' 'Yes,' I replied. 'Must not everyone who reads it identify with her? And you have to remember that not only is she ashamed of what she said to Miss Bates, but that she would rather anyone in the world had heard her saying it than Mr Knightley, whom she now begins to know she loves.' The girls were amazed. They asked if this kind of sentimental self-indulgence were really what I read novels for. Did I not realise that texts were there to be deconstructed? Did I really believe that a text, any text, bore any relation to a world outside itself? Perhaps I did not understand that the reader makes the meanings in the text, and there is no single truth contained in them. I realised I had fallen among disciples of Derrida, and that not only further conversation about *Emma* but further conversation about Truth in Art was impossible.

But we had to keep going for an hour. So I told them about one of Sartre's arguments to prove that solipsism is impossible, that we cannot possible doubt that other people exist. For we know that we exist as objects in their eyes. His argument, like so many in *Being and Nothingness*, takes the form of a story. (Sartre was the most novelistic, or theatrical of philosophers.) A man, moved by curiosity or jealousy, bends down outside the door where his wife is talking to someone, and listens at the keyhole. The man is completely absorbed in this activity of trying to hear, and is unselfconscious. But suddenly he hears a footstep. Someone has come into the hall behind him. He is observed as an eavesdropper, and he is conscious of himself in shame. The undeniable existence of shame proves that we are not alone in the world. We live not only for ourselves, but as characters in other people's lives. Therefore other people exist.

This is an argument, if one is needed, against solipsism. (I have never personally been persuaded of the need of such arguments.) But it is also an argument depending on our instant understanding of what it is to be ashamed of ourselves. So it shows not only that other people exist, but that other people are recognisably like ourselves; they experience the same emotions in the same sort of circumstances. I suggested to my pupils both that it is, as Sartre believed, a fact about the real world that shame exists, but also that Sartre, had he known of it, could equally well have proved his point by the story of the picnic on Box Hill.

We hear a great deal of talk about our multicultural society, about constructing our own meanings, as my pupils told me, and about the ephemeral and relative nature of moral concepts and other values. But this is not the whole, nor the most important part of the truth. There is a huge central area of values shared by human beings, things that are nice or nasty, good, bad or ridiculous, and remain so across the centuries wherever human beings exist. Nothing makes this more comfortingly manifest than reading and rereading Jane Austen.

Fay Weldon

novelist and screenwriter

❦

It may seem extraordinary that a brief romantic novel written by a 22-year-old girl in 1797 keeps making it into the lists of great masterworks (it came in at no. 36 in the *Sunday Times* Millennium Masterworks poll). It tells an unpretentious and improbable tale of how an impoverished country girl, by virtue of her spirit and vivacity, captures the heart, title and estates of a great lord. The novel is, of course, Jane Austen's *Pride and Prejudice*, written under the title 'First Impressions', rejected sight unseen by a London publisher, rewritten and retitled by Austen when she was thirty-two, after which it was briskly published by sensible John Murray. The ten extra years would no doubt have sharpened her wits and honed her style: she was not to have all that many more of them – she died when she was forty-one.

But I bet that famous first sentence, 'It is a truth universally acknowledged, that a single man in possession of a good fortune, must be in want of a wife', was there in the first version. It rings with the zest and excitement of the young novelist setting out for the first time with a tale to tell and a whatever-next view of the world. The novel adds up to far more than the sum of its parts, which is why teachers of English Literature so love it: and why, what with the low-cut dresses, and its good clear archetypal characters – from Mrs Bennet the foolish mother to Mr Collins the pompous clergyman – it's such a doddle for television and film adaptation. It contains the message we want to hear: what does a girl need of rank, fame, face or fortune – if she has a wry, dry wit, some dignity and a cheerful disposition? As for Elizabeth Bennet, so for Jane Austen herself.

The novel, which attracted little attention at the time, stretches beyond the great rambling mid-Victorian novels of Thackeray, Dickens, Eliot and the Brontës, to reach its natural inheritors in the mid-twentieth century: the shaped, ironic, elegantly constructed works of, say, Evelyn Waugh and Graham Greene. She got there first. And, of course, it's not what you say it's the way that you say it that counts. A kitchen-maid plot – but then so was Brontë's *Jane Eyre*, and we forgive that. In the light of Austen's cool, distinctive prose all doubts subside. It all came so naturally, so easily and so young, that is the marvel: and with such exhilaration. Look, she seems to be saying to the reader, in this story, in these few pages, I can confirm for you the whole world as I know it, all the subtleties of social and sexual interplay: the argument ongoing through the centuries of what's right and what's wrong; what's prudence and what's folly.

Pride and Prejudice contains the nub of what was to be explored in Austen's more complex, more mature novels – six in all – reflecting and informing a change in social mores, as the arranged and loveless marriages of women gave way to the notion of marriage as an expression of love and desire.

Pity Jane Austen if you must, this maiden lady without children or sexual experience. But she would have known the exhilaration of the writer when she put down her pen after *Pride and Prejudice*. I bet she knew that what she'd written would outrun the generations.

The Sunday Times, 17 October 1999

Rebecca West

novelist and journalist

❦

To believe her limited in range because she was so harmonious in method is as sensible as to imagine that when the Atlantic Ocean is as smooth as a mill-pond it shrinks to the size of a mill-pond. There are those who are deluded by the decorousness of her manner, by the fact that her virgins are so virginal that they are unaware of their virginity, into thinking that she is ignorant of passion. But look through the lattice-work of her neat sentences, joined together with the bright nails of craftsmanship, painted with the gay varnish of wit, and you will see women haggard with desire or triumphant with love, whose delicate reactions to men make the heroines of all our later novelists seem merely to turn signs, 'Stop' or 'Go' toward the advancing male. And the still sillier reproach, that Jane Austen has no sense of the fundamental things in life, springs from a misapprehension of her place in time. She came at the end of the eighteenth century, when the class to which she belongs was perhaps more intelligent than it has ever been before and since, when it had dipped more deeply than comfortable folk have ever done into philosophical enquiry. Her determination not to be confused by emotion, and to examine each phenomenon of the day briskly and on its merits, was never a sign of limitation. It was a sign that she lived in the same world as Hume and Gibbon.

The Strange Necessity, 1928

Ann Widdecombe
Shadow Home Secretary

❦

One of Austen's great attractions is that she portrays such a calm and ordered world. No matter how great the whirlwind of emotions, hopes and disappointments her heroines are suffering, manners are meticulously observed, routine is unaffected. Everybody and everything has a place and is always to be found neatly there. You would never think there was a war raging as her characters agonise over the finer points of propriety and which young ladies are out.

It is all a perfect escape for a politician who divides her life between shouting down a disorderly chamber, chasing up the loose ends of policy, sorting out (or at least trying to) the most awful muddles on behalf of constituents and confounding the Government.

Yet not for the world would I change places with an Austenian character. Imagine trimming hats all day while waiting for the likes of that conceited ass, Darcy, to propose!

Hugo Williams

poet

❧

My father[1] was the first Mr Darcy on the stage of the St James's Theatre, St James's Street, in the early 1930s opposite Celia Johnson. Both actors are dead now and the theatre long ago demolished. But my brother married Celia's daughter Lucy Fleming and they look just like the photos of my father and Celia on the playbill of *Pride and Prejudice*. My father's lovely blue set of Jane Austen's novels is missing *Pride and Prejudice*, because lost by me as a boy.

1. Hugh Williams, the actor and playwright

Leonard Woolf

publisher

❦

Dear Mrs Kamiya,

I was reading a novel of Jane Austen when something struck me which I thought might be of interest to you in your work on Virginia, though I feel it is rather presumptuous on my part, as a layman, to write to you who are an expert. However the point is this. In *Pride and Prejudice* and in several of the other novels there is a very lively-minded young woman – the heroines in *Pride and Prejudice* and in *Emma*, who are completely mistaken about some person and important question, and yet in the end see their mistake, fall in love and are loved, and live happily ever after. I think these characters are unconsciously Jane herself, who obviously from her books and letters, had this kind of lively, critical and witty and ironical mind. She never married and one can see that she would have frightened off most young men and would have turned down on her side most of them. It seems to me the mistake and ultimate success of her heroines is a kind of compensation daydream for her failure in real life.

I seem to see the same thing in one phenomenon in Virginia's books. In real life she had some complex about food. When she was insane she refused to eat altogether and even when well she had a curious complex about food, for it was always difficult to get her to eat enough to keep her well. Yet she really enjoyed food in a perfectly normal way though she would not like to admit this. The curious thing is that food plays a very important part in her books, e.g. the elaborate description of Boeuf en Daube in *To the Lighthouse* and the importance of the lunches in *A Room of One's Own.* Is there not a kind of compensation here too, the admission of the liking for and importance of food in fiction which was irrationally suppressed or denied in actual life.

I hope you don't mind my suggesting this.

Yours sincerely,
Leonard Woolf

Letter to Miyeko Kamiya, June 1967

Virginia Woolf

novelist

❦

More than any other novelist she fills every inch of her canvas with observation, fashions every sentence into meaning, stuffs up every chink and cranny of the fabric until each novel is a little living world, from which you cannot break off a scene or even a sentence without bleeding it of some of its life. Her characters are so rounded and substantial that they have the power to move out of the scenes in which she placed them into other moods and circumstances. This, if some one begins to talk about Emma Woodhouse or Elizabeth Bennet voices from different parts of the room being saying which they prefer and why, and how they differ and how they might have acted if one had been at Box Hill and the other at Rosings, and where they live, and how their houses are disposed, as if they were living people. It is a world, in short, with houses, roads, carriages, hedgerows, copses, and with human beings.

All this was done by a quiet maiden lady who had merely paper and ink at her disposal; all this is conveyed by little sentences between inverted commas and smooth paragraphs of print. Only those who have realized for themselves the ridiculous inadequacy of a straight stick dipped in ink when brought into contact with the rich and tumultuous glow of life can appreciate to the full the wonder of her achievement, the imagination, the penetration, the insight, the courage, the sincerity which are required to bring before us one of those perfectly normal

90

and simple incidents of average human life. Besides all these gifts and more wonderful than any of them, for without it they are apt to run to waste, she possessed in a greater degree perhaps than any other English woman the sense of the significance of life apart from any personal liking or disliking; of the beauty and continuity which underlies its trivial stream. A little aloof, a little inscrutable and mysterious, she will always remain, but serene and beautiful also because of her greatness as an artist.

The Times Literary Supplement, 8 May 1913

I have just got the Austen letters – I was so much irritated by that article that I thought I must see if there wasn't a good deal more in them than he or she made out.

I find as I suspected that the man or woman is entirely wrong, and that the Austen letters are so important and interesting that I fear I shall have to write about them one of these days myself. And, again, Ethel dear, you're entirely wrong – whatever 'Bloomsbury' may think of JA, she is not by any means one of my favourites. I'd give all she ever wrote for half of what the Brontës wrote – if my reason did not compel me to see that she is a magnificent artist.

The letters are to me fascinating – for what they don't say largely.

I'm reading Jane Austen [Letters] in this heavenly solitude over the log fire: and whether its my luxurious state,

91

anyhow I find her steadily improve. I think her little fame at the end brisked her up – good Lord, she died at 42: the best to come.

Sequence of letters to Ethel Smyth, November–December 1932, on first publication of Jane Austen's Letters

Afterword

🍎

Not everybody invited to contribute to this volume was able to do so, generally owing to the demands made by work on busy lives. Some of those who did not, however, sent charming and gracious replies, several of them almost as amusing as the items from contributors. In one or two cases, the very succinctness of the refusal was a delight in itself: the editor of a national newspaper who wrote 'I am terribly sorry but I have never really been a fan of Jane Austen' was only slightly less laconic than the distinguished novelist who put on the back of a picture postcard 'Sorry. Nowt useful to say. Good luck'. Some were frank about not being swept along in what it is all too easy to assume is a universal tide of Austenthusiasm: 'I'm afraid that Jane Austen is one of those subjects on which I have nothing to say, so I must ask you not to expect anything from me'. In others there was an apologetic note: 'To my shame, I have to confess I have never read and studied Jane Austen as I know I should have done; so, alas, I feel that I have nothing of moment or interest to contribute.' A number of people attested to their enjoyment of the books, but felt that, as one put it, not being a particular Jane Austen 'buff', their views would be of little help.

Nevertheless Jane's spirit seemed to be hovering somewhere above these disclaimers. An elegant sentence in a letter from a famous playwright might almost have come from her own pen: 'I am sorry to disappoint you but I'm afraid I have nothing to send for your millennium volume other than my best wishes for its success'. While the correspondent who wrote crisply 'Sorry, I can't come up with a Jane-bite' seemed disconcertingly to see through the entire enterprise.

The most endearing refusal came from a grand old man of letters who wrote 'I wish I could help you with your book, but I am too old and too dotty to do so.' And the most encouraging was undoubtedly 'It's an excellent idea and I shall be among the first to buy the book.'

To all those who wrote to us, whether they sent something for inclusion or simply their good wishes, we express our sincere thanks.

Acknowledgements

❧

The Jane Austen Society is grateful for the collaboration of Chawton House Library in supporting the production of this book. The 'Great House' and landscape at Chawton which Jane Austen loved are being restored. Chawton will house the Centre for the Study of Early English Women's Writing (1600–1830) and a unique collection of rare books. Initiated by the Leonard X. Bosack and Bette M. Kruger Foundation in America, Chawton House Library is now seeking support to complete the restoration and refurbishment of the splendid manor house, its gardens and park.

The editors are grateful to all those authors and publishers who have kindly given their permission to reproduce material in this volume. Every effort has been made to trace copyright holders but we should be delighted to include in subsequent editions any whom we have not been able to find.

W.H. AUDEN: *Collected Longer Poems* (Faber & Faber, 1968); JOHN BAYLEY: in *A Passion for Books*, ed. Dale Salwak (Macmillan, 1999); QUENTIN BELL: *Elders and Betters* (John Murray, 1995); ALAN BENNETT: *Writing Home* (Faber & Faber, 1994); ARNOLD BENNETT: *The Evening Standard Years* (Evening Standard/Solo Syndication, 1974); ELIZABETH BOWEN: *English Novelists* (Collins, 1945); LORD DAVID CECIL: *Poets and Story-tellers* (Constable, 1949); BRUCE CHATWIN: in Nicholas Shakespeare, *Bruce Chatwin* (The Harvill Press in association with Jonathan Cape, 1999); G.K. CHESTERTON: *The Victorian Age in Literature* (Oxford University Press, 1913); SIR WINSTON CHURCHILL: *The Second World War* (Cassell, 1952); IVY COMPTON-BURNETT: 'A Conversation' in Charles Burkhart, *The Art of I. Compton-Burnett* (Gollancz, 1972); Hilary Spurling, *Secrets of a Woman's Heart: the later life of I. Compton-Burnett,* (Hodder & Stoughton, 1984); MARGARET DRABBLE: Introduction to *Pride and Prejudice* (Virago, 1989); RONALD DUNCAN: *Working with Britten: A Personal Memoir* (The Rebel Press, 1981; by permission of The Ronald Duncan Literary Foundation); E.M. FORSTER: *Aspects of the Novel,* (Edward Arnold, 1927; by permission of The Provost and Scholars of King's College, Cambridge and The Society of Authors); STELLA GIBBONS: in Reggie Oliver, *Out of the Woodshed* (Bloomsbury, 1998); RUPERT HART-DAVIS: *The Lyttleton Hart-Davis Letters,* volume II (John Murray, 1979); P.D. JAMES: *Time to be in Earnest: a fragment of autobiography* (Faber & Faber, 1999); SELMA JAMES: *The Ladies and the Mammies* (Falling Wall Press, 1983); PHILIP LARKIN: *Selected Letters of Philip Larkin*, ed. Anthony Thwaite (Faber & Faber, 1992); D.H. LAWRENCE: *The Letters of D.H. Lawrence*, ed. Aldous Huxley (Heinemann, 1932); F.R. LEAVIS, *The Common Pursuit* (Chatto & Windus, 1952 ; by permission of the Executors of the F.R. Leavis Estate); DAVID LODGE: copyright © David Lodge, first published in the

Guardian, 1999; GEORGE LYTTLETON, *The Lyttleton Hart-Davis Letters*, Volumes I and III (John Murray, 1978, 1981); HAROLD MACMILLAN: *Riding the Storm 1956-59* (Macmillan, 1971); KATHERINE MANSFIELD: *The Letters of Katherine Mansfield*, ed. John Middleton Murry (Constable, 1928); W. SOMERSET MAUGHAM: *Ten Novels and their Authors* (Heinemann, 1954; by permission of Random House); ELLEN MOERS: *Literary Women* (The Women's Press, 1978); VLADIMIR NABOKOV: *Lectures on Literature* (Weidenfeld & Nicolson, 1980); NIGEL NICOLSON: adapted from *Long Life* (Weidenfeld & Nicolson, 1997); WILLIAM PLOMER: reprinted in *Electric Delights*, ed. Rupert Hart-Davis (Jonathan Cape, 1978); BEATRIX POTTER: Margaret Lane, *The Tale of Beatrix Potter* (Frederick Warne, 1946; by permission of Penguin Books Ltd); J.B. PRIESTLEY: *Literature and Western Man* (Heinemann, 1962); BARBARA PYM: *A Very Private Eye: an Autobiography in Letters and Diaries*, ed. Hazel Holt and Hilary Pym (Macmillan, 1984); DOROTHY L. SAYERS: *The Letters of Dorothy L. Sayers*, ed. Barbara Reynolds, Volumes I and III (Hodder & Stoughton, 1995, 1998); FREYA STARK: *Freya Stark Letters*, ed. Lucy Moorhead (Compton Russell, 1976); REBECCA WEST: *The Strange Necessity* (Jonathan Cape, 1928; reprinted Virago Press, 1987); LEONARD WOOLF: *The Letters of Leonard Woolf*, ed. Frederic Spotts (Bloomsbury, 1990); VIRGINIA WOOLF: *The Sickle Side of the Moon: the Letters of Virginia Woolf 1932-35*, ed. Nigel Nicolson and Joanne Trautmann (Chatto & Windus, 1979).